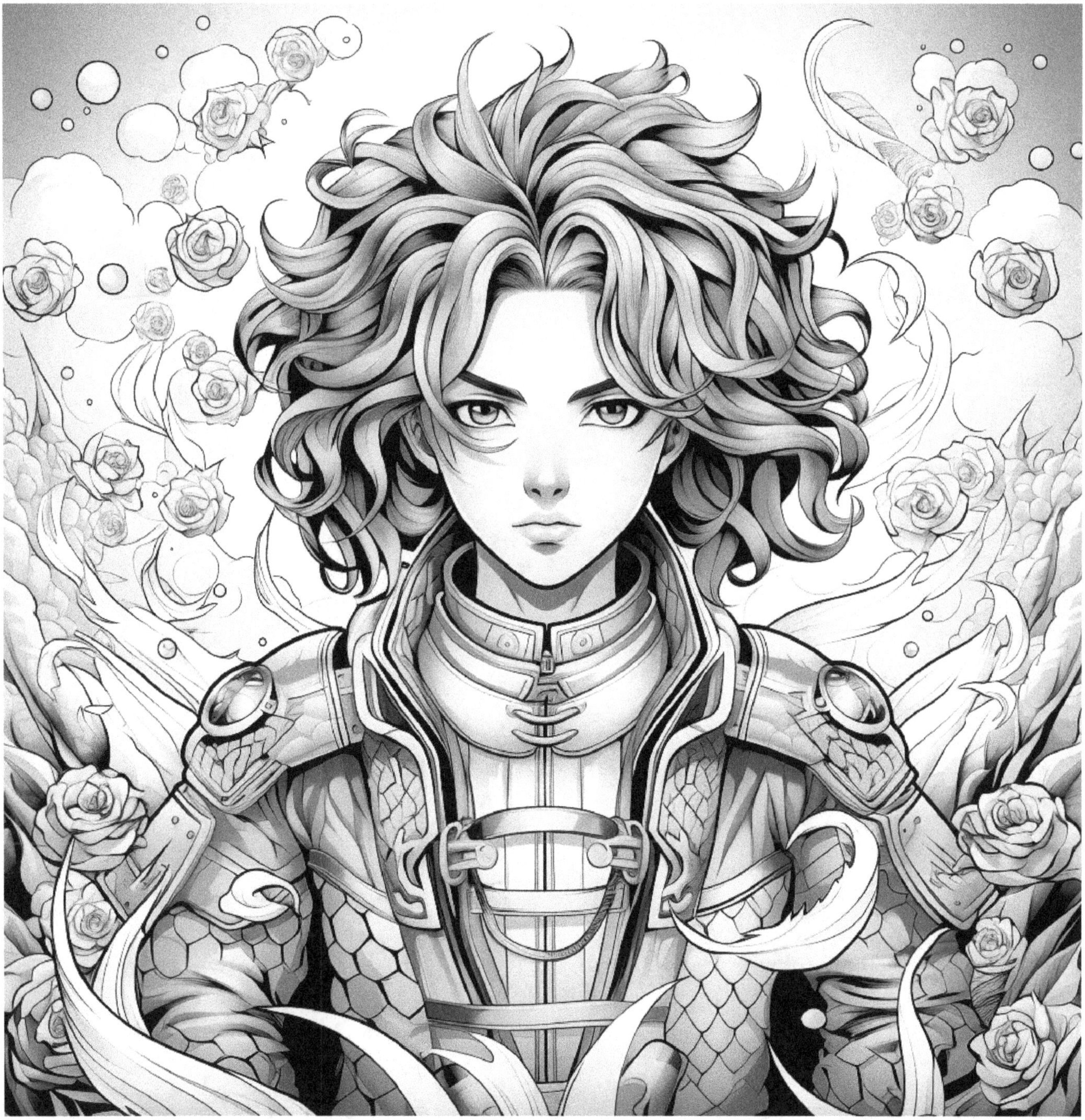

THIS COLORING BOOK BELONGS TO:

____

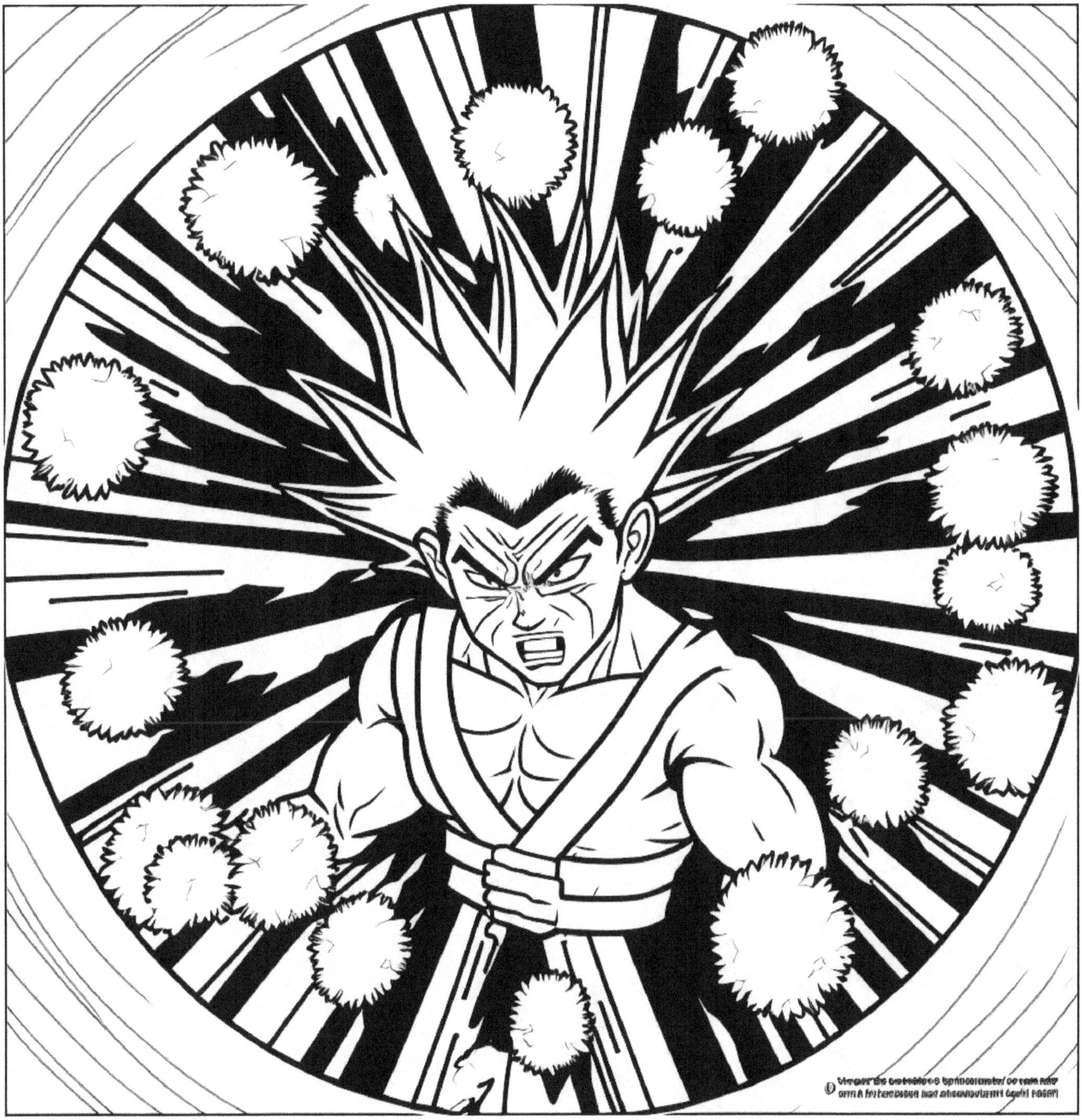

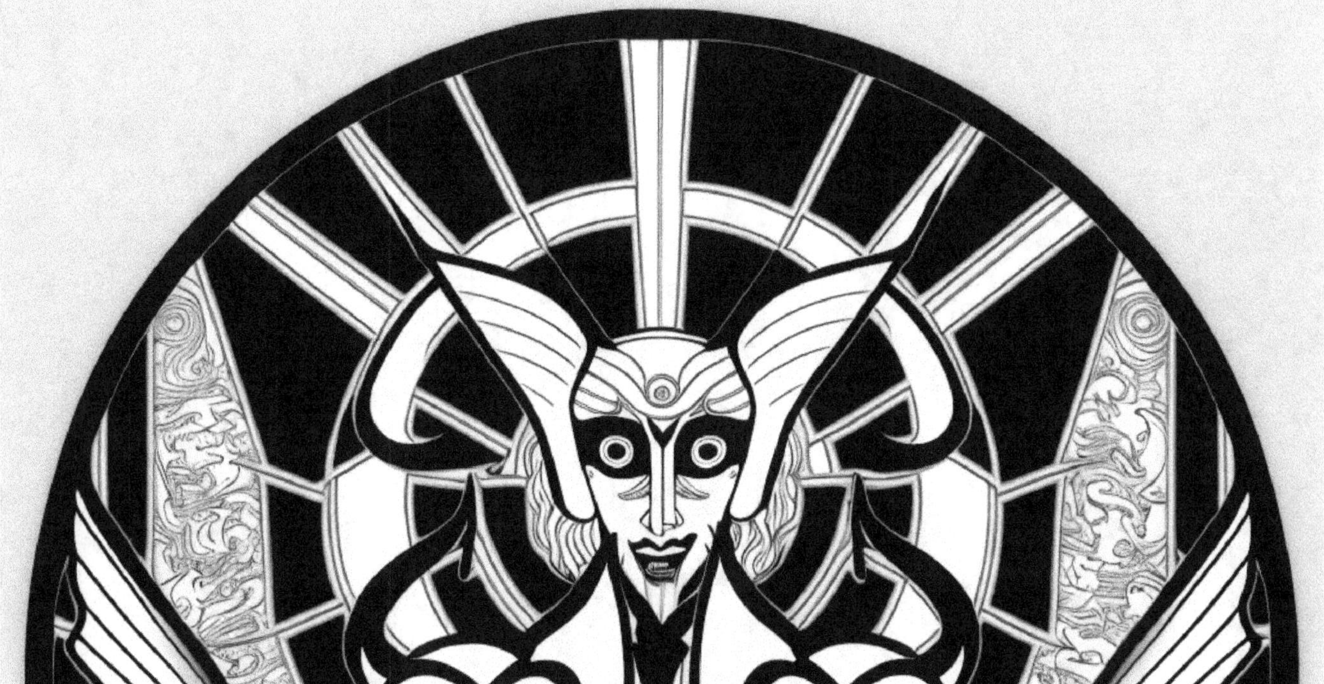

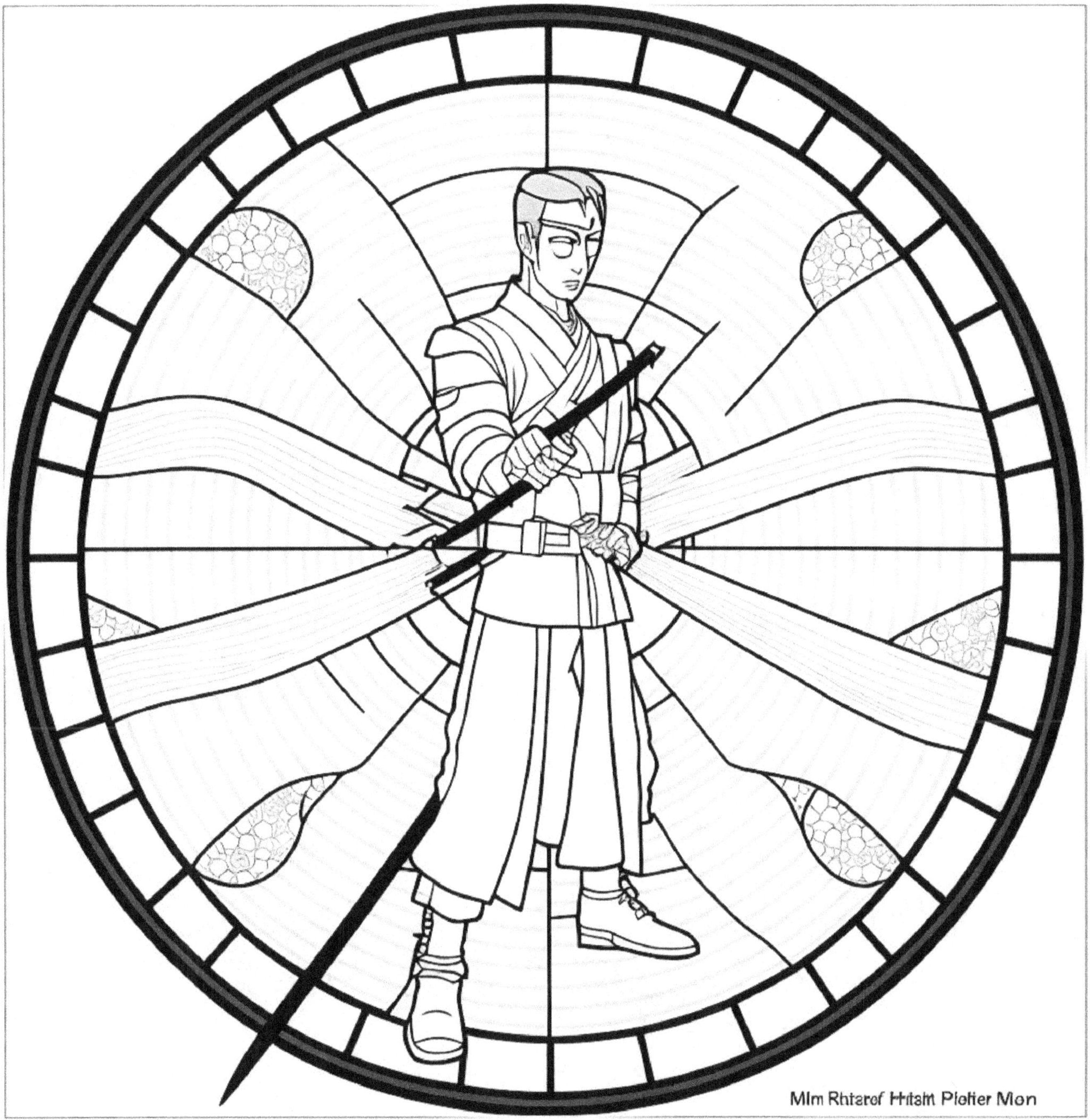
Mlm Rhtaref Hrtsm Pletier Mon

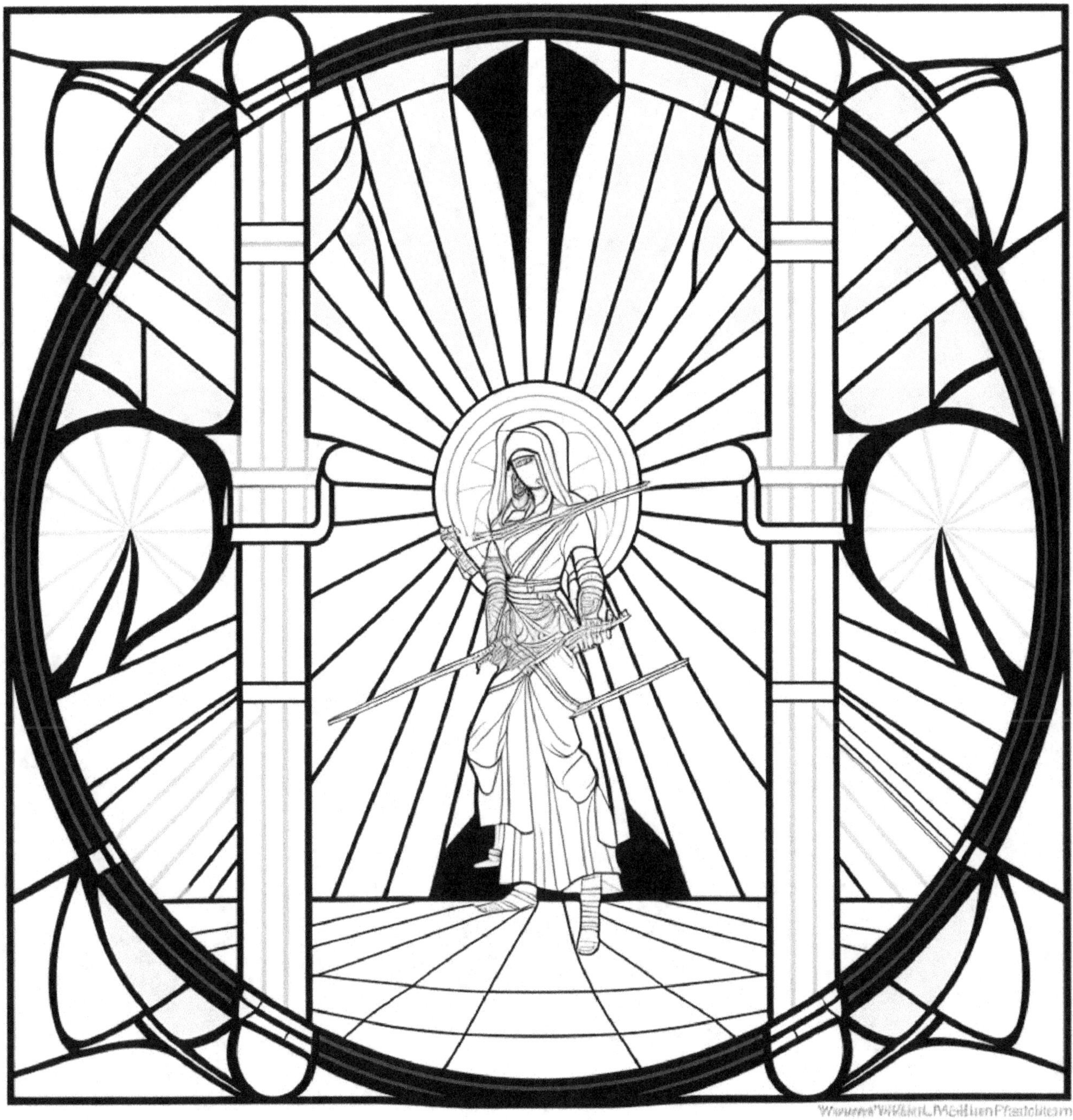

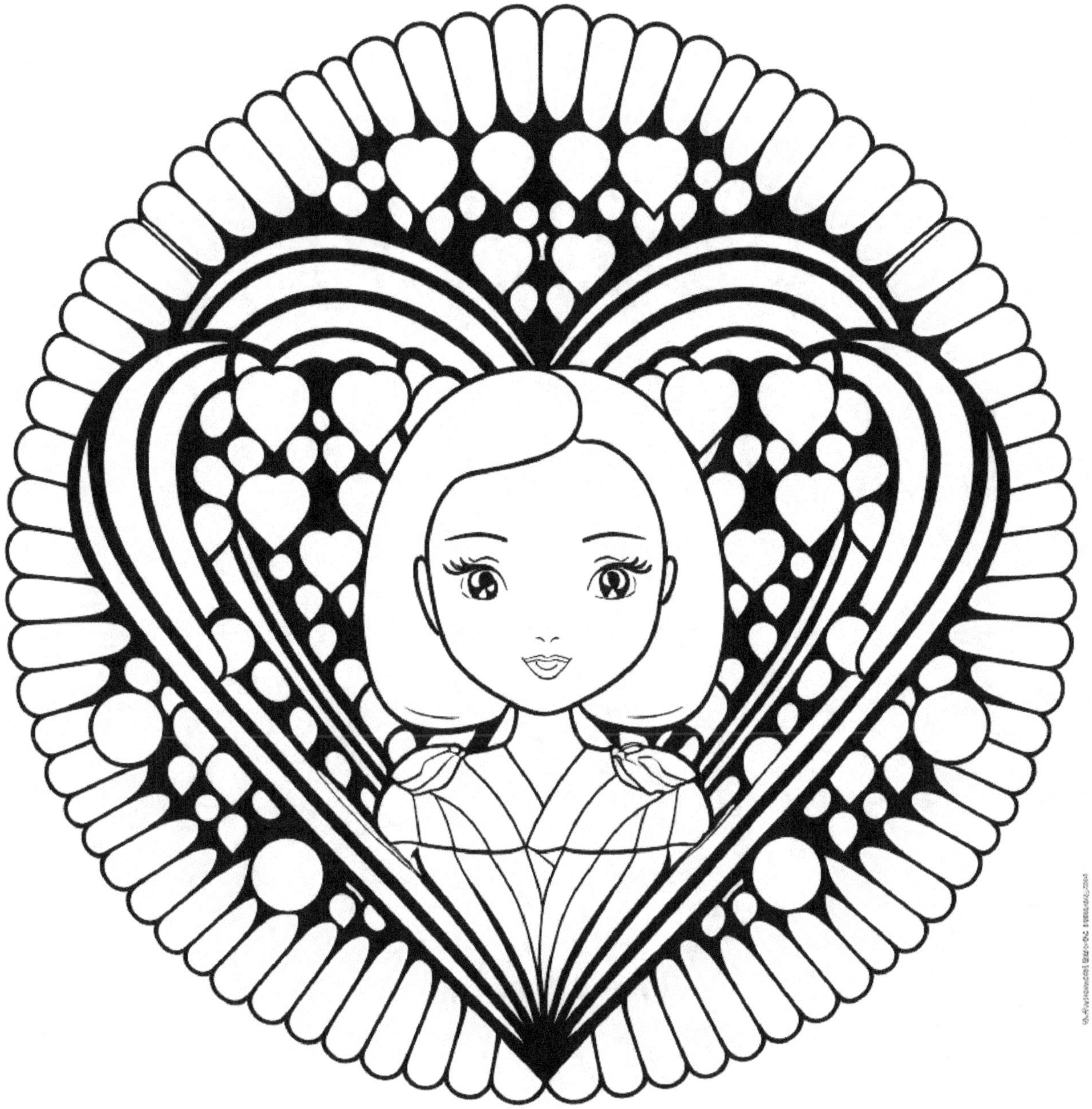

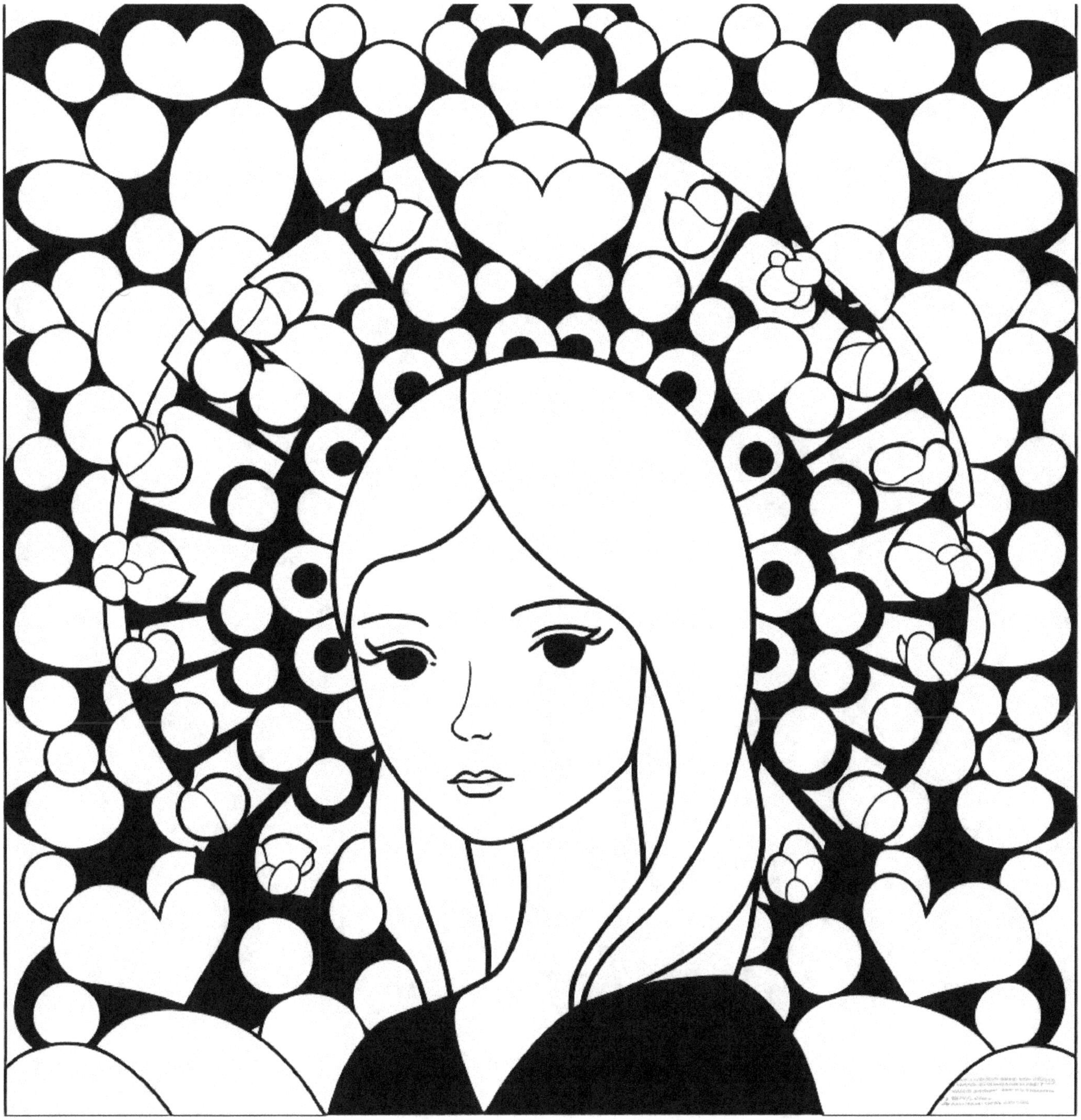

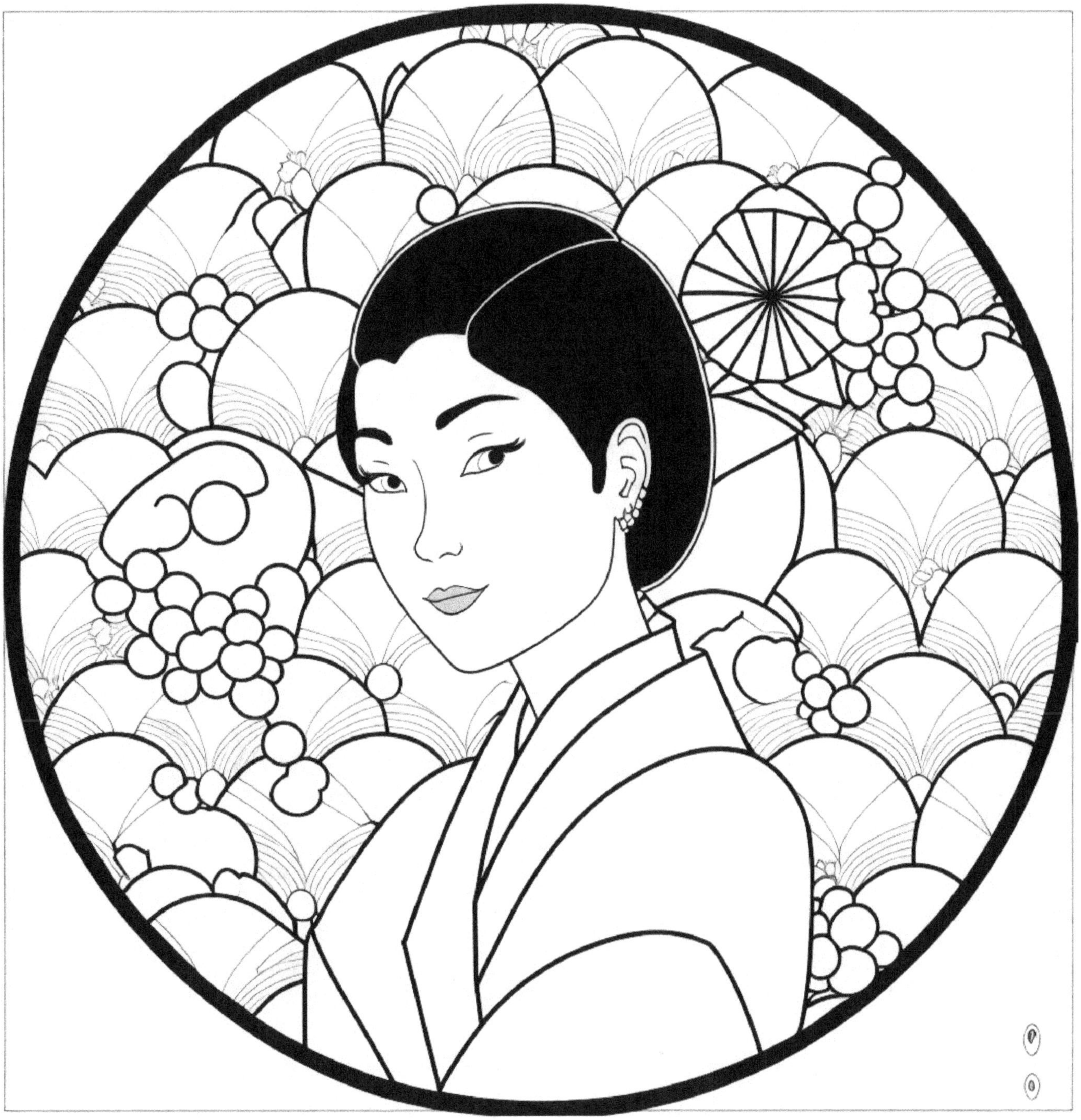

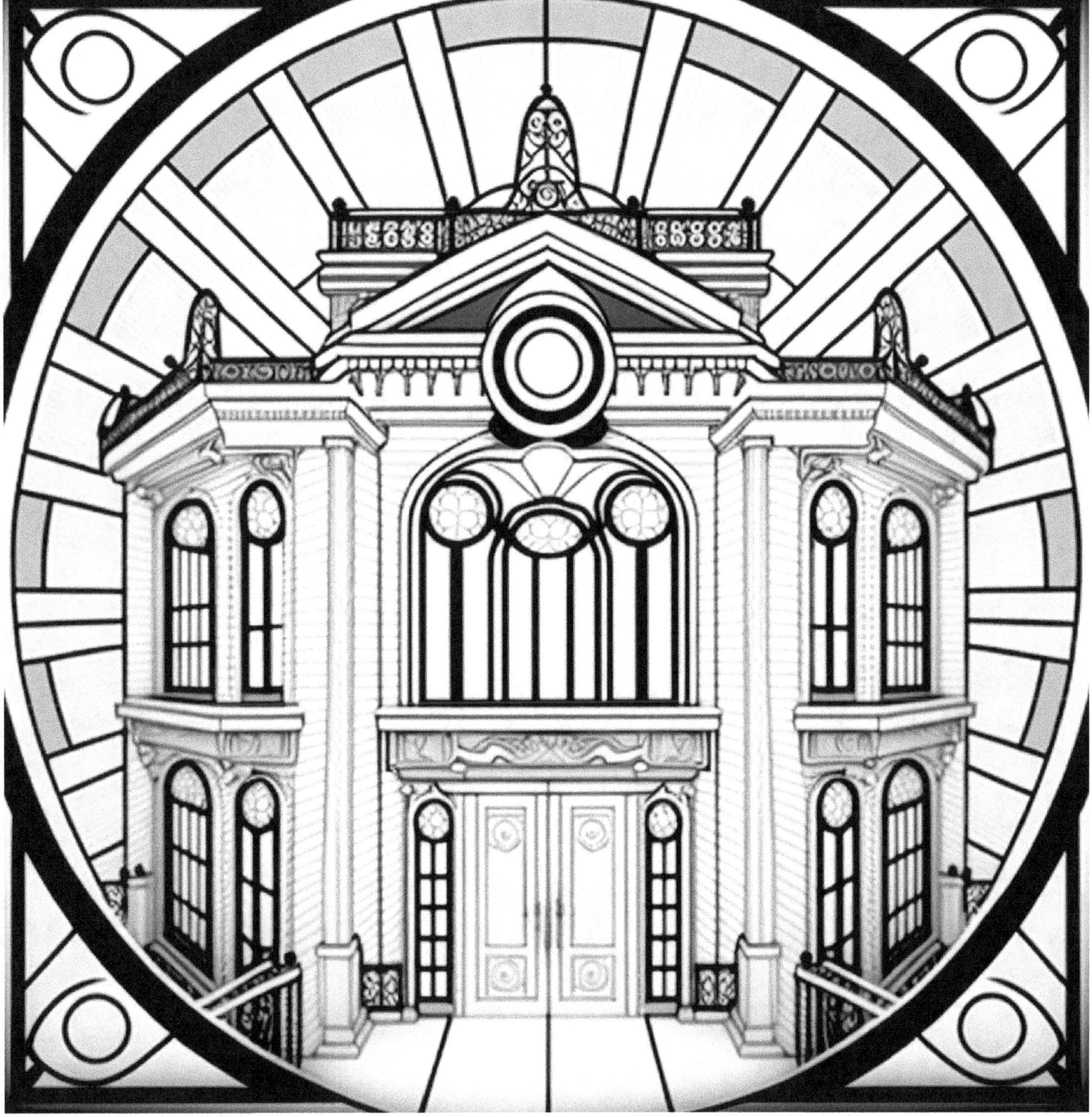

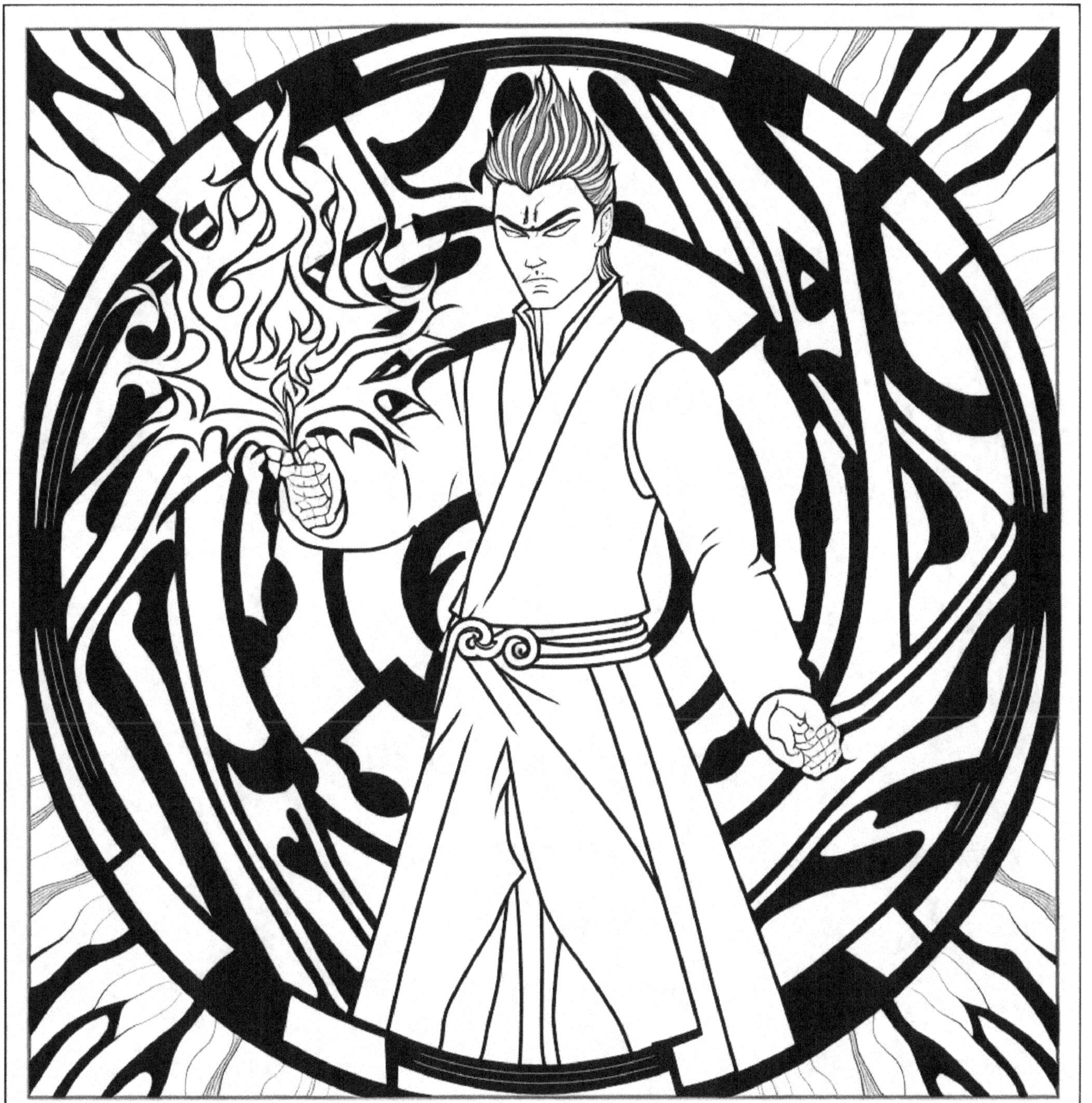

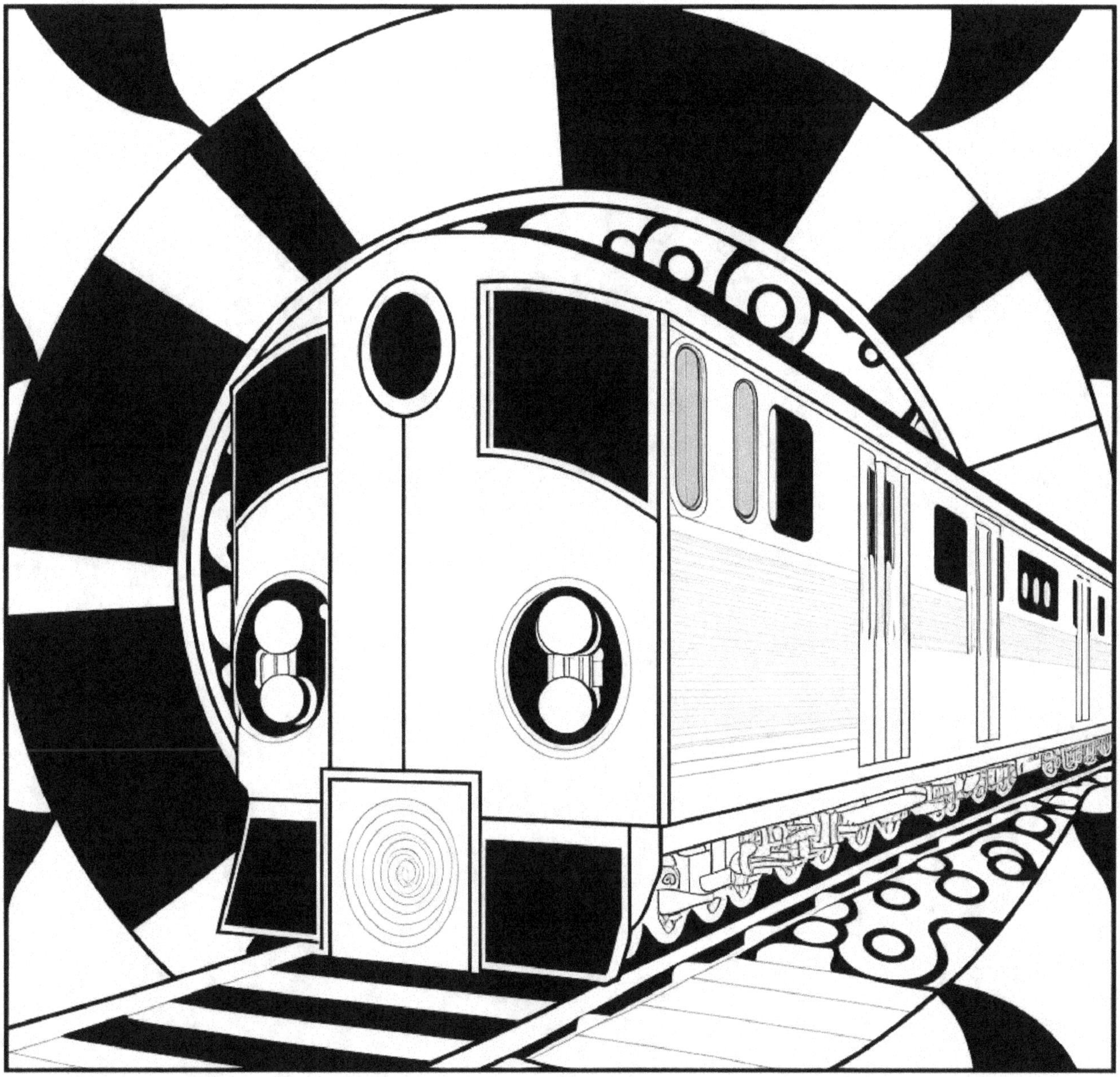

Juirignrion Ginaimg Darging

lieirne HK Shoehdkarto

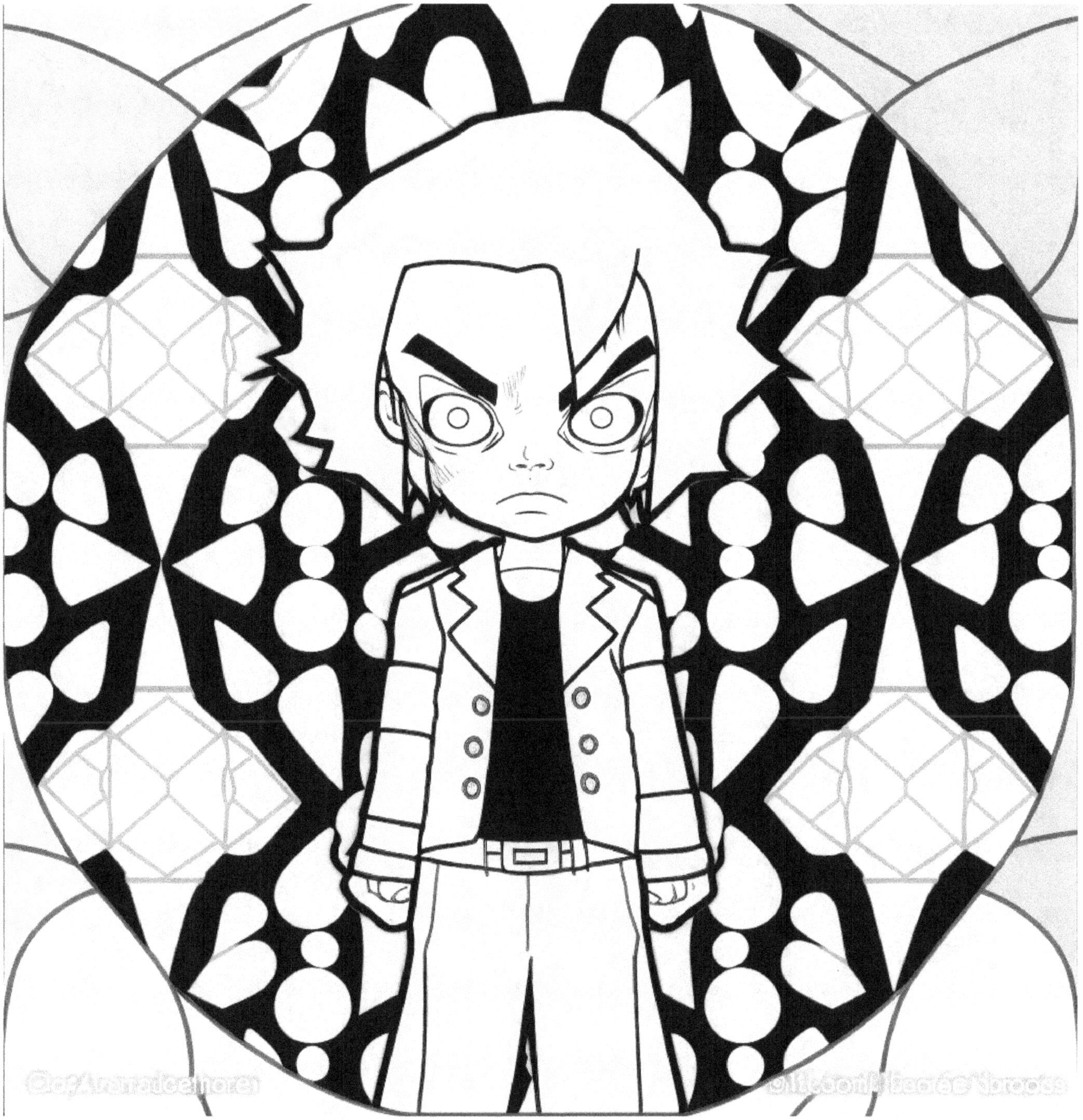

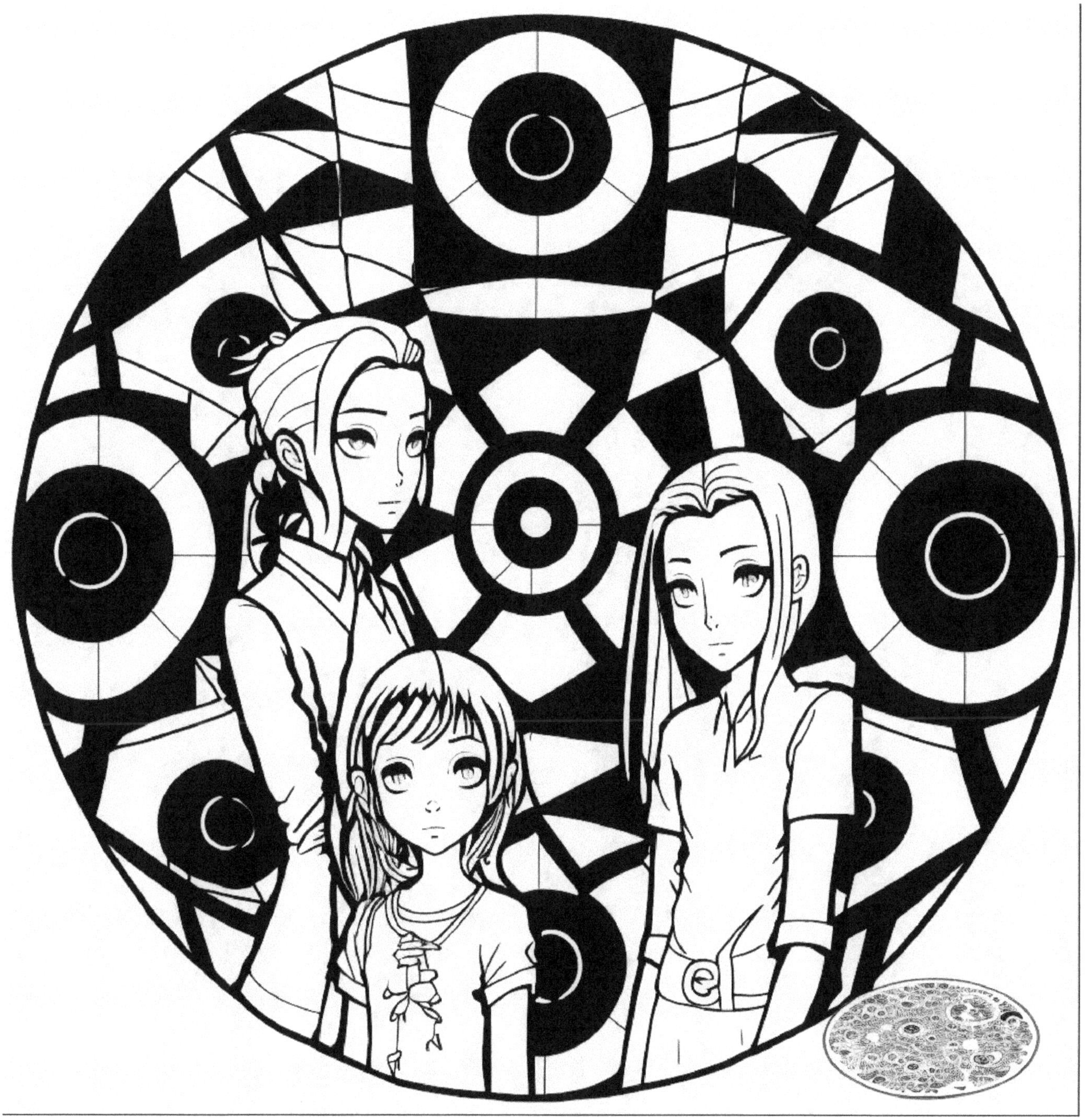

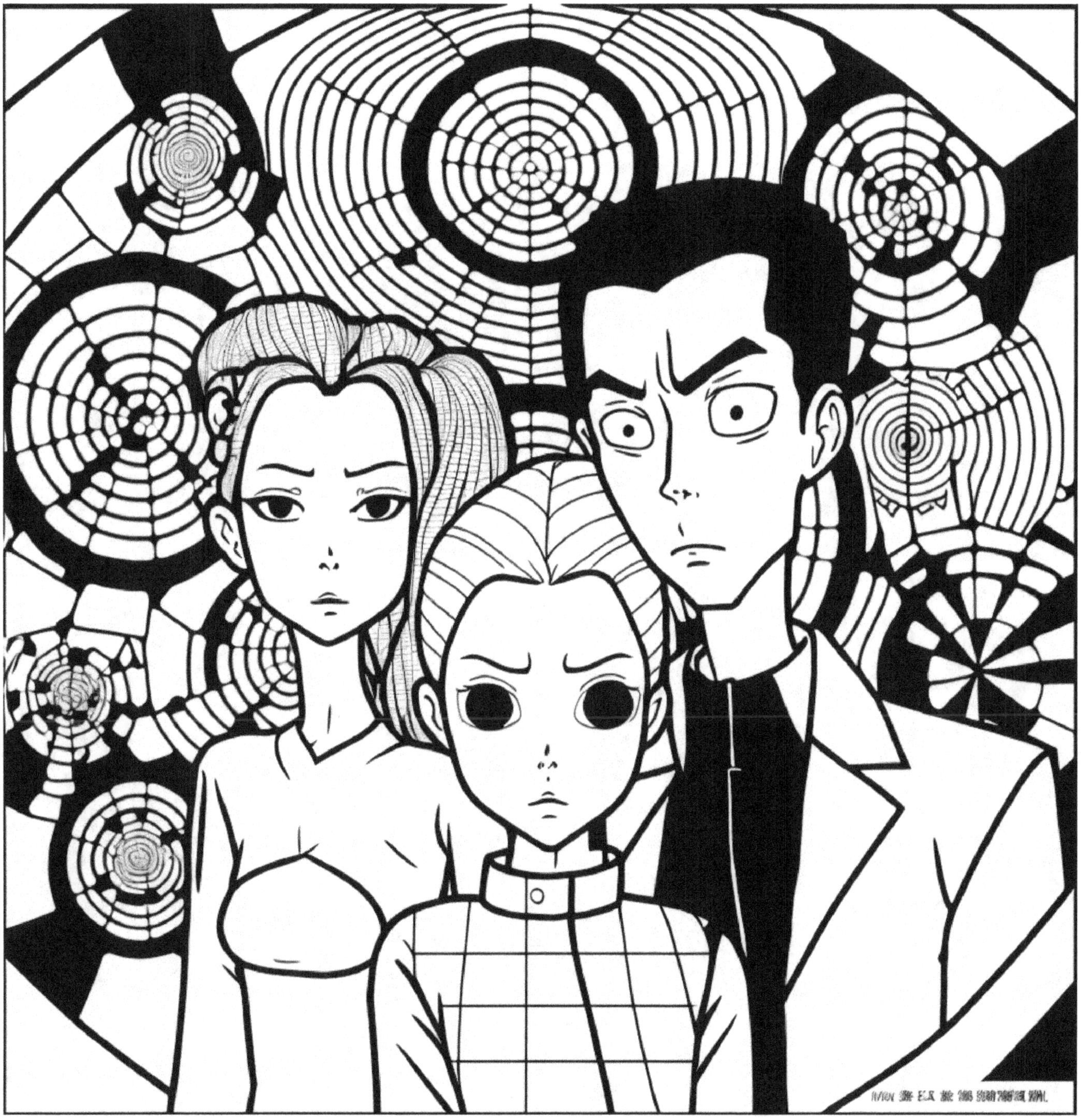

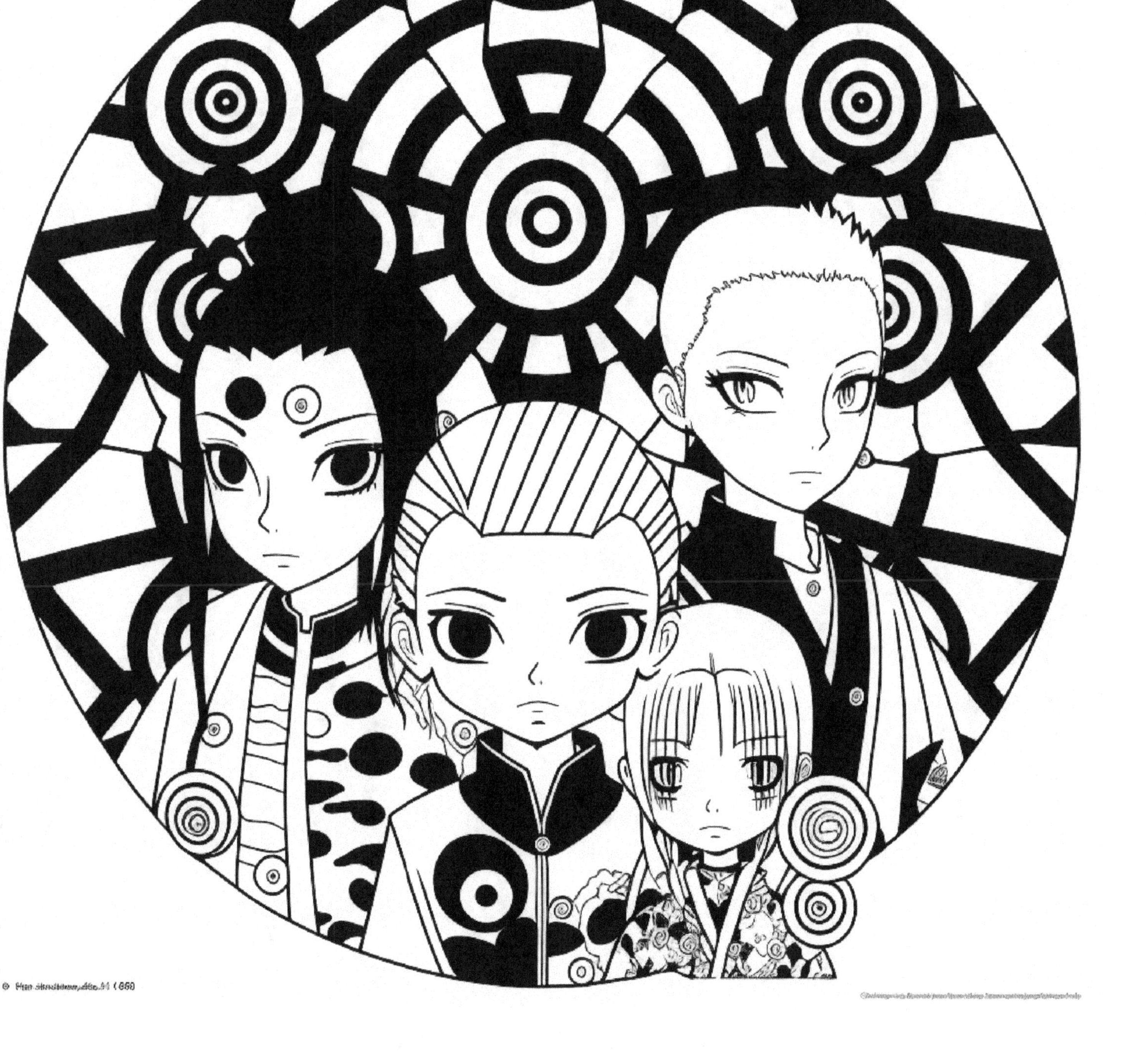

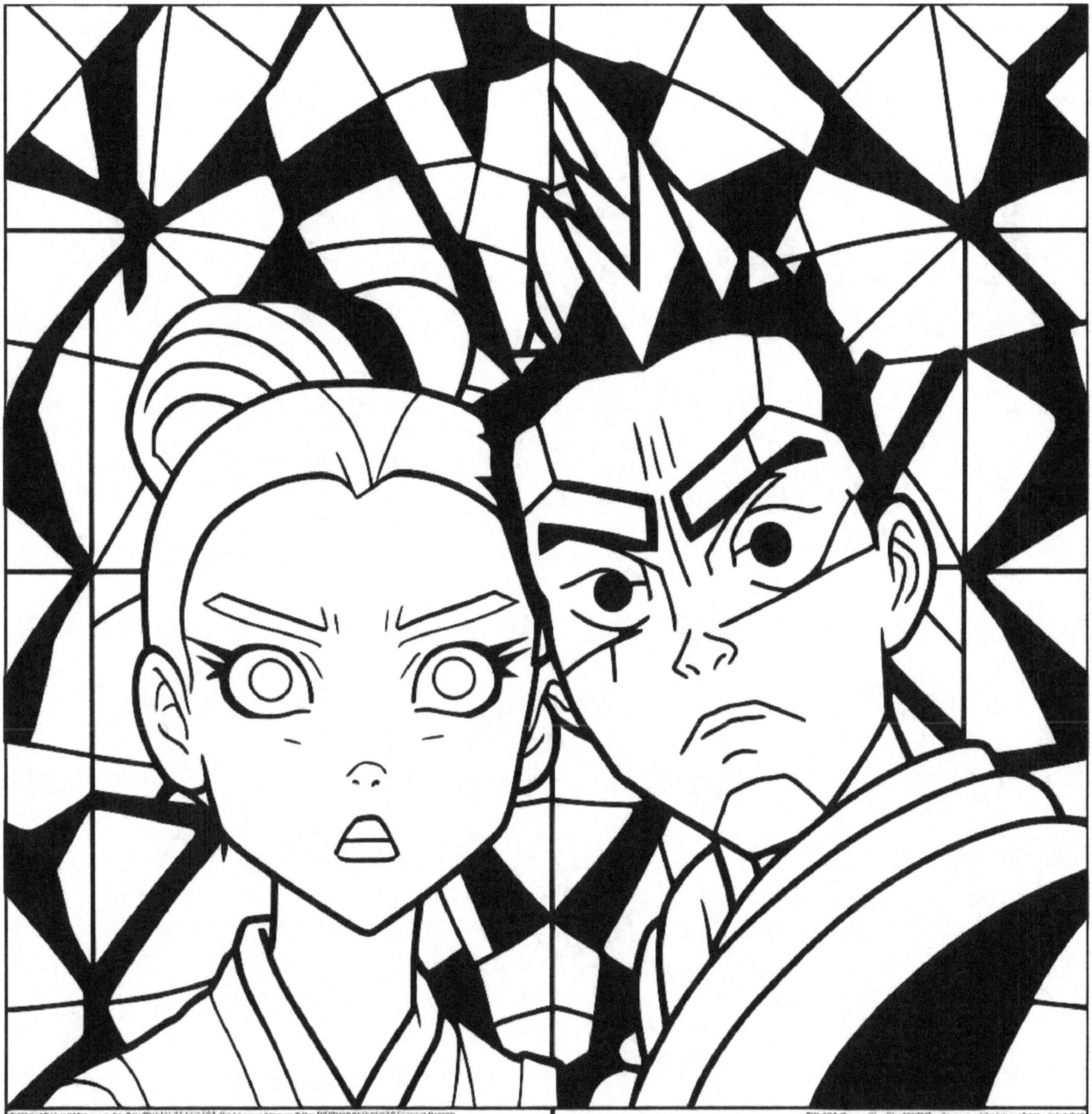

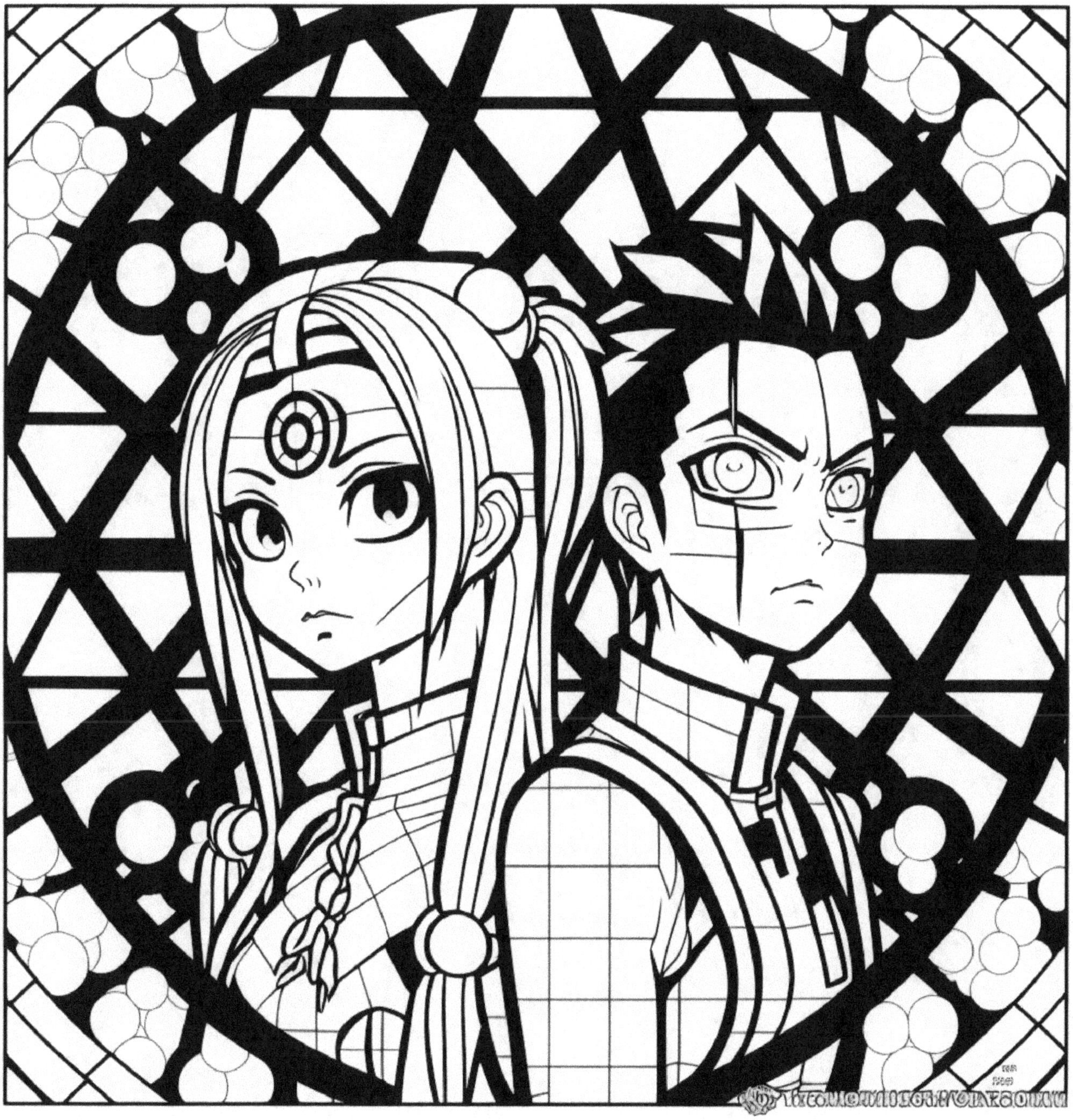

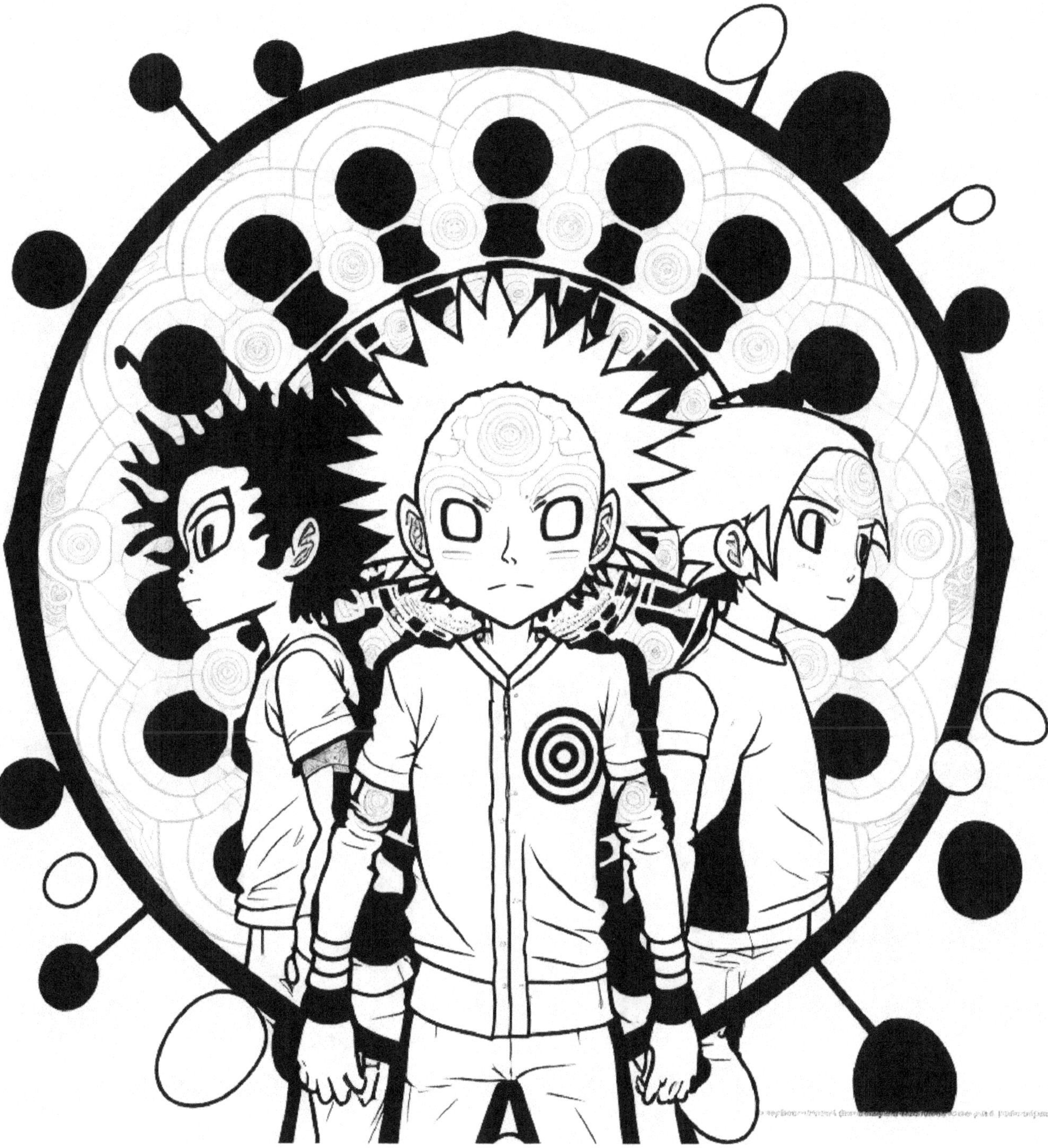

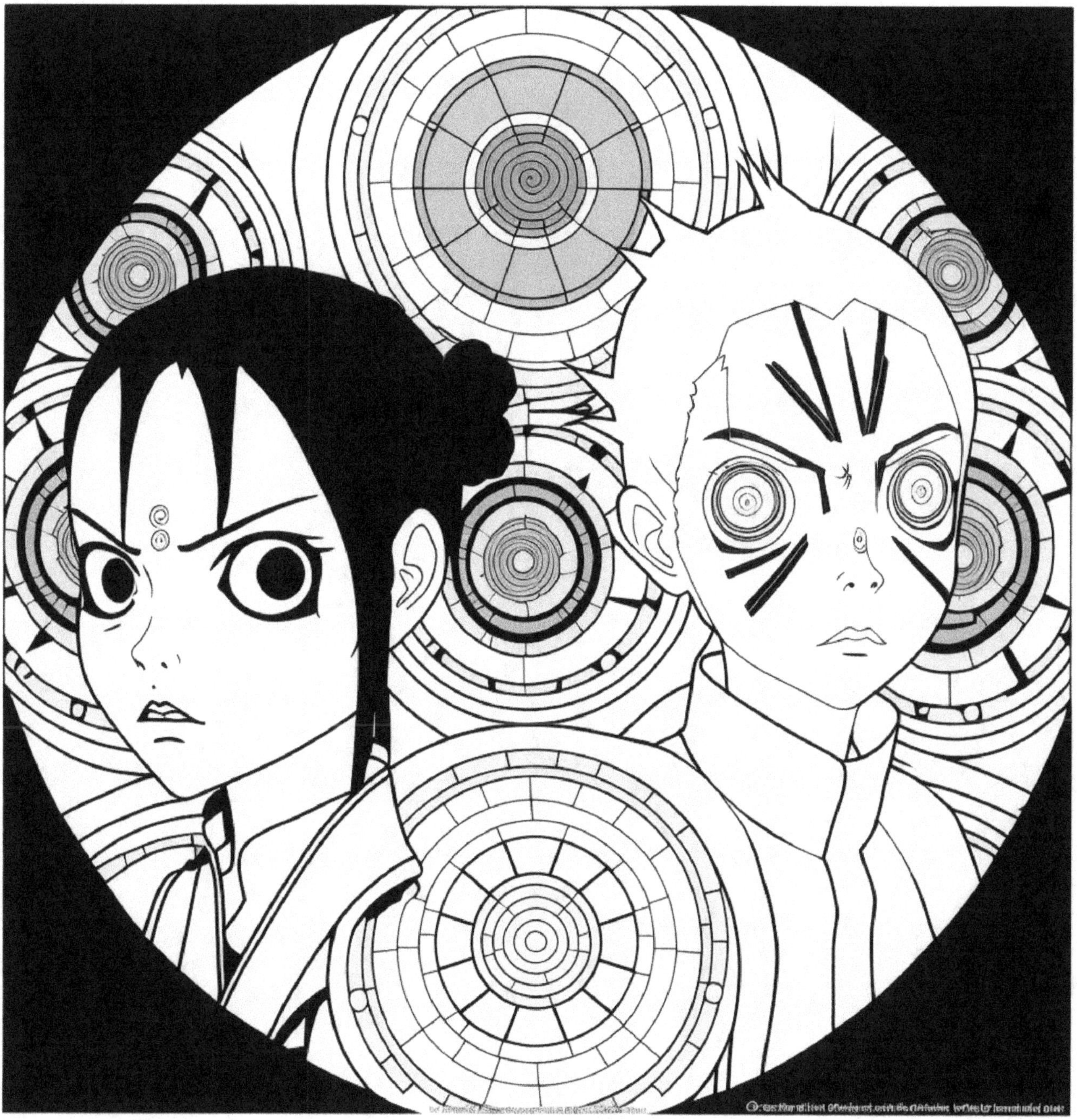

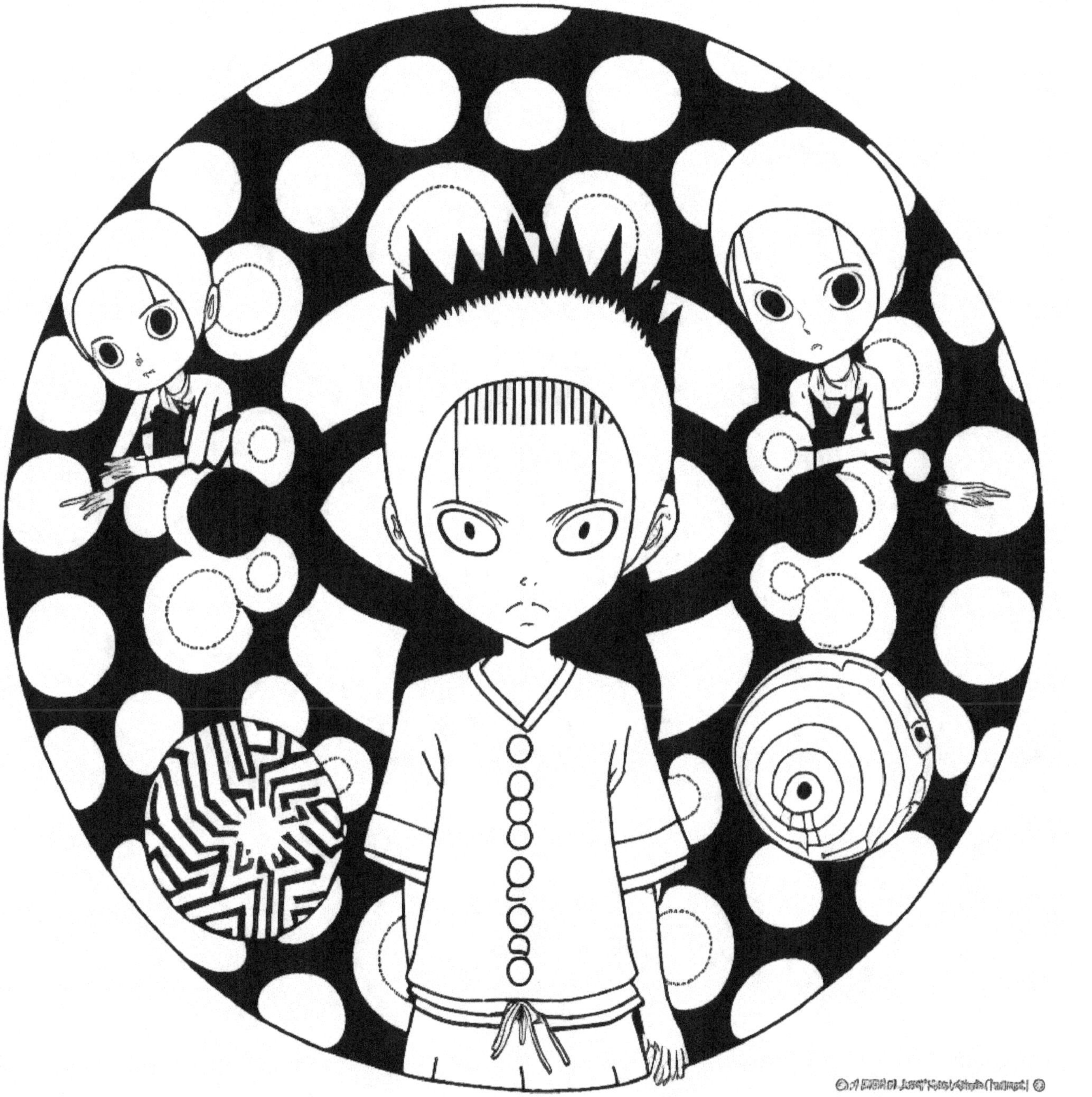

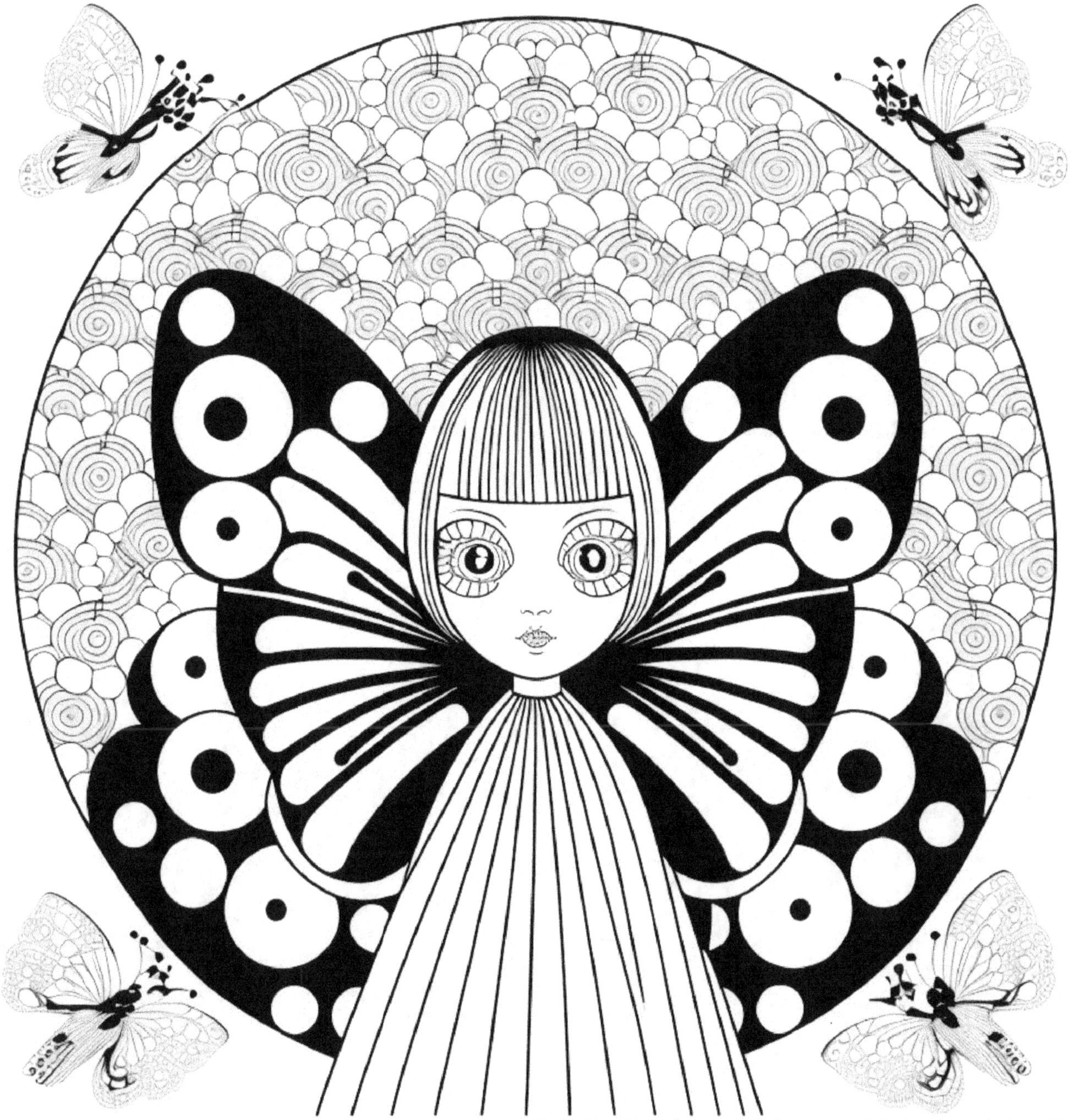

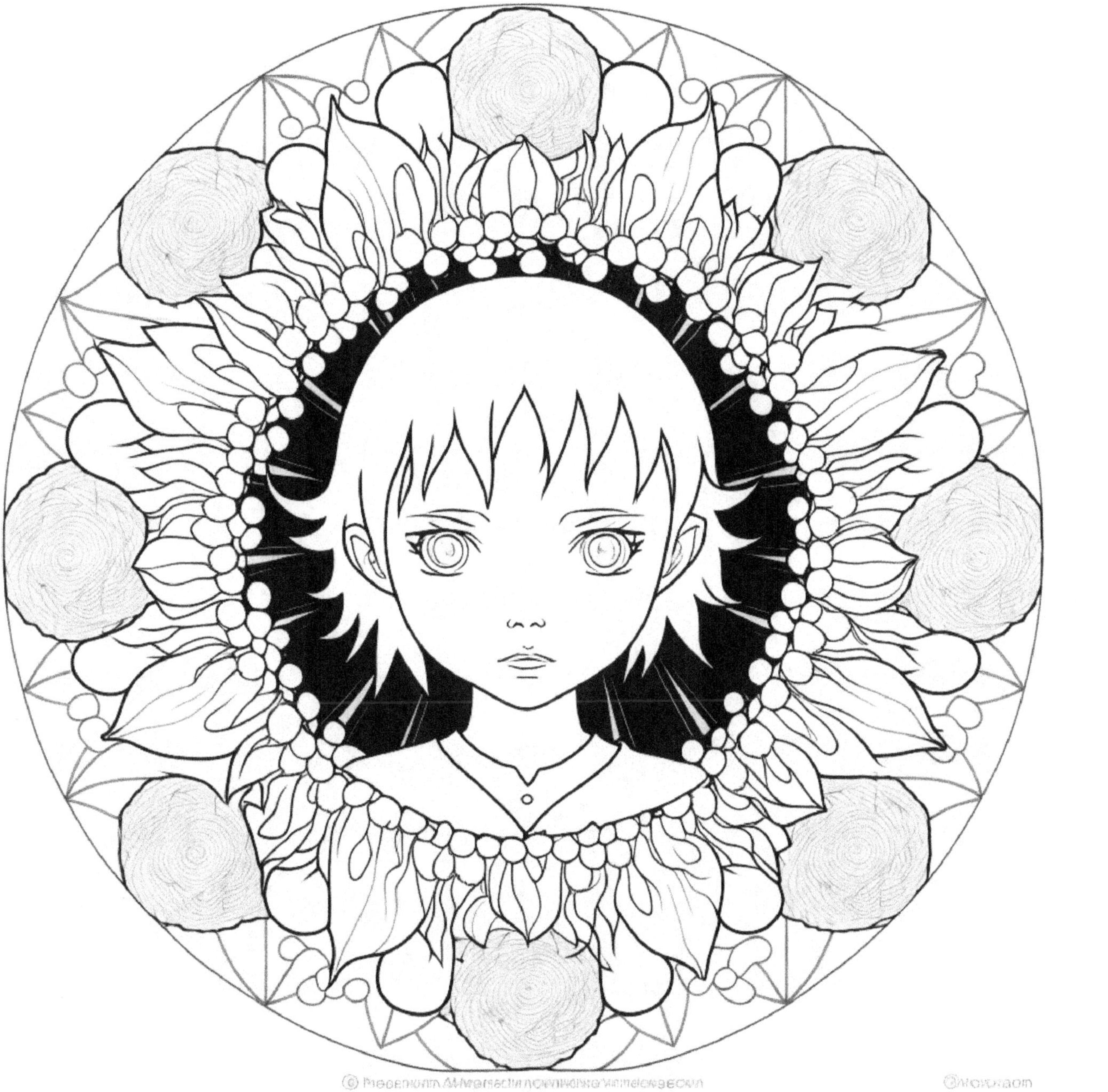

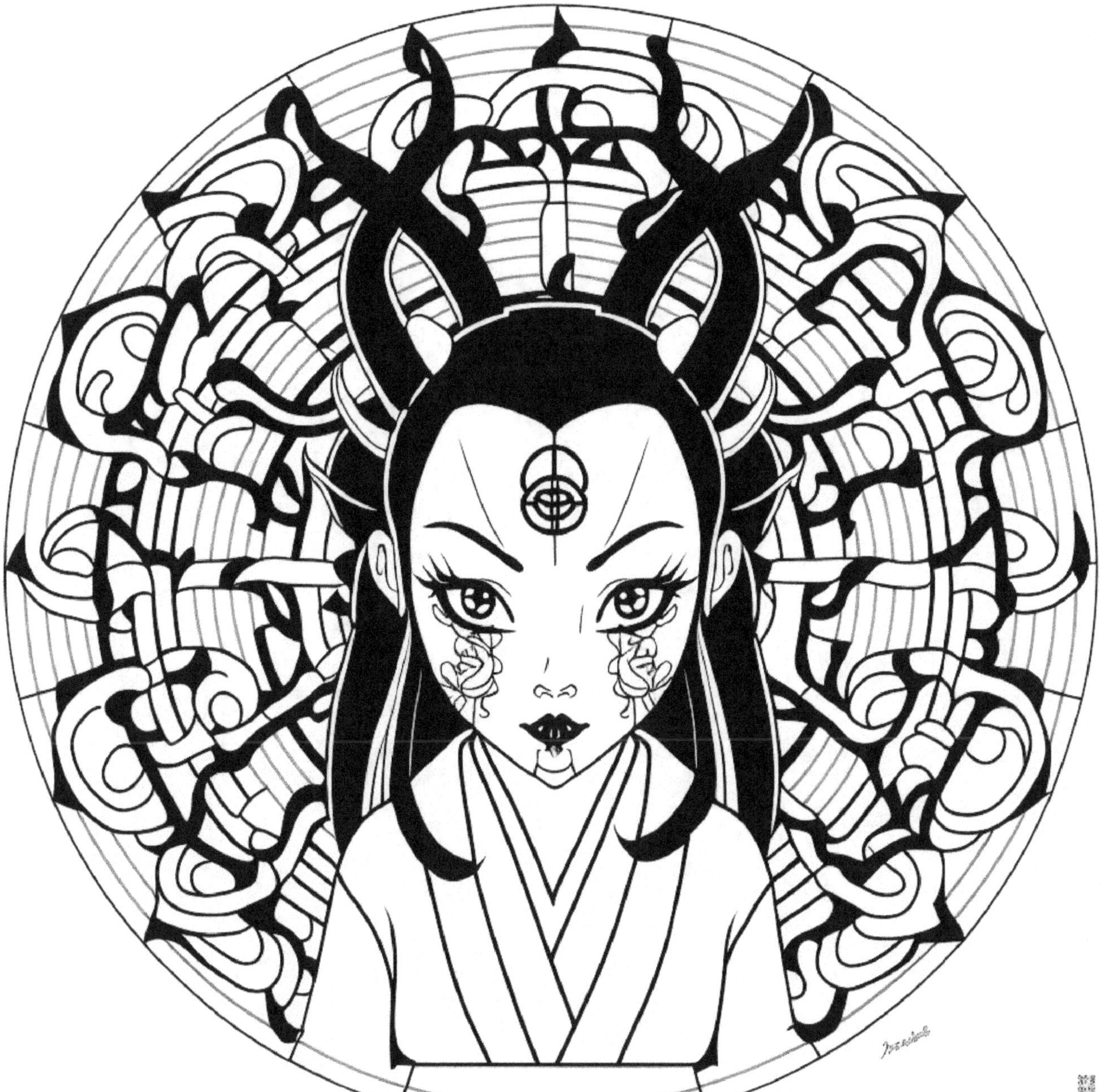

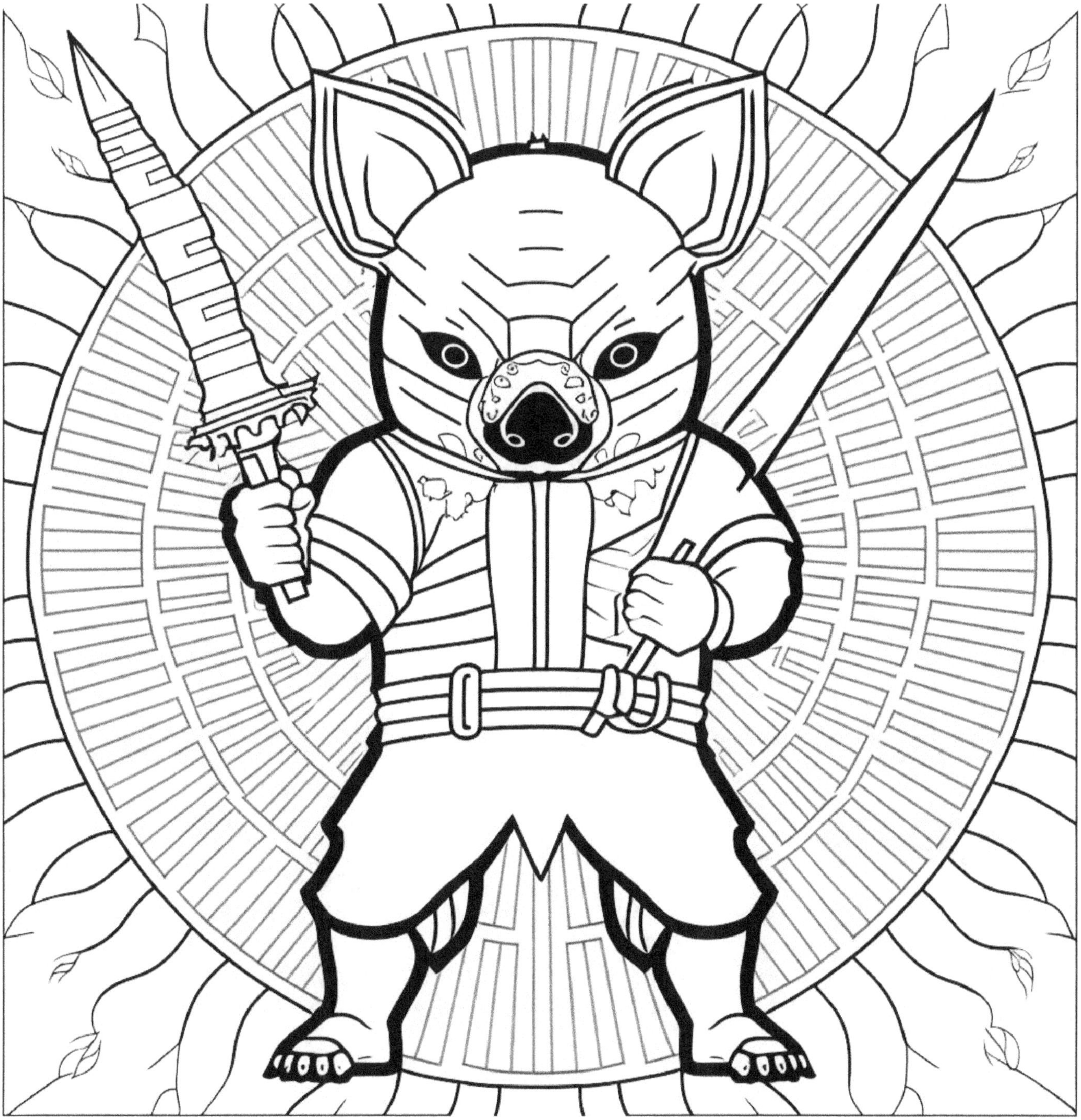

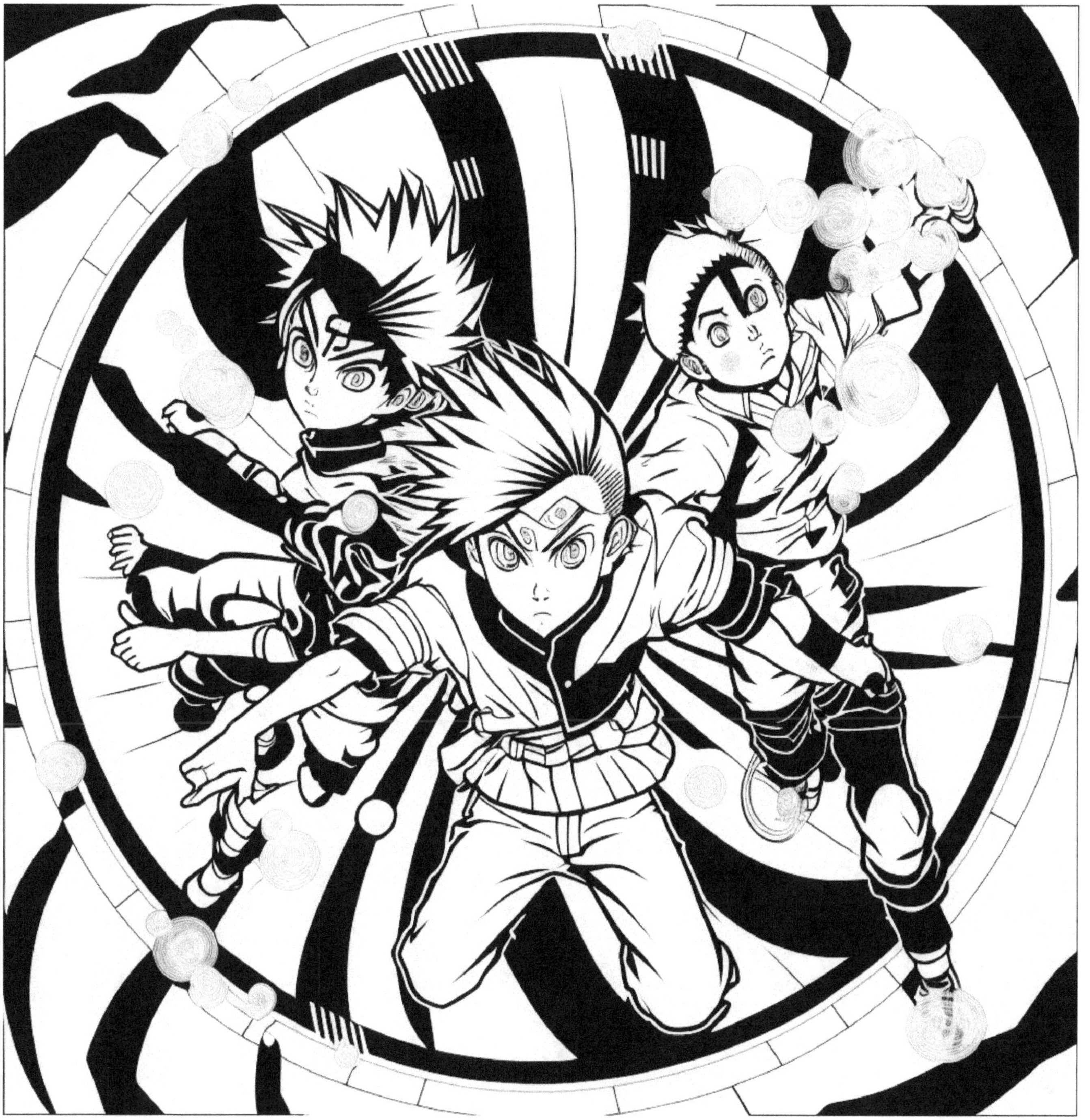

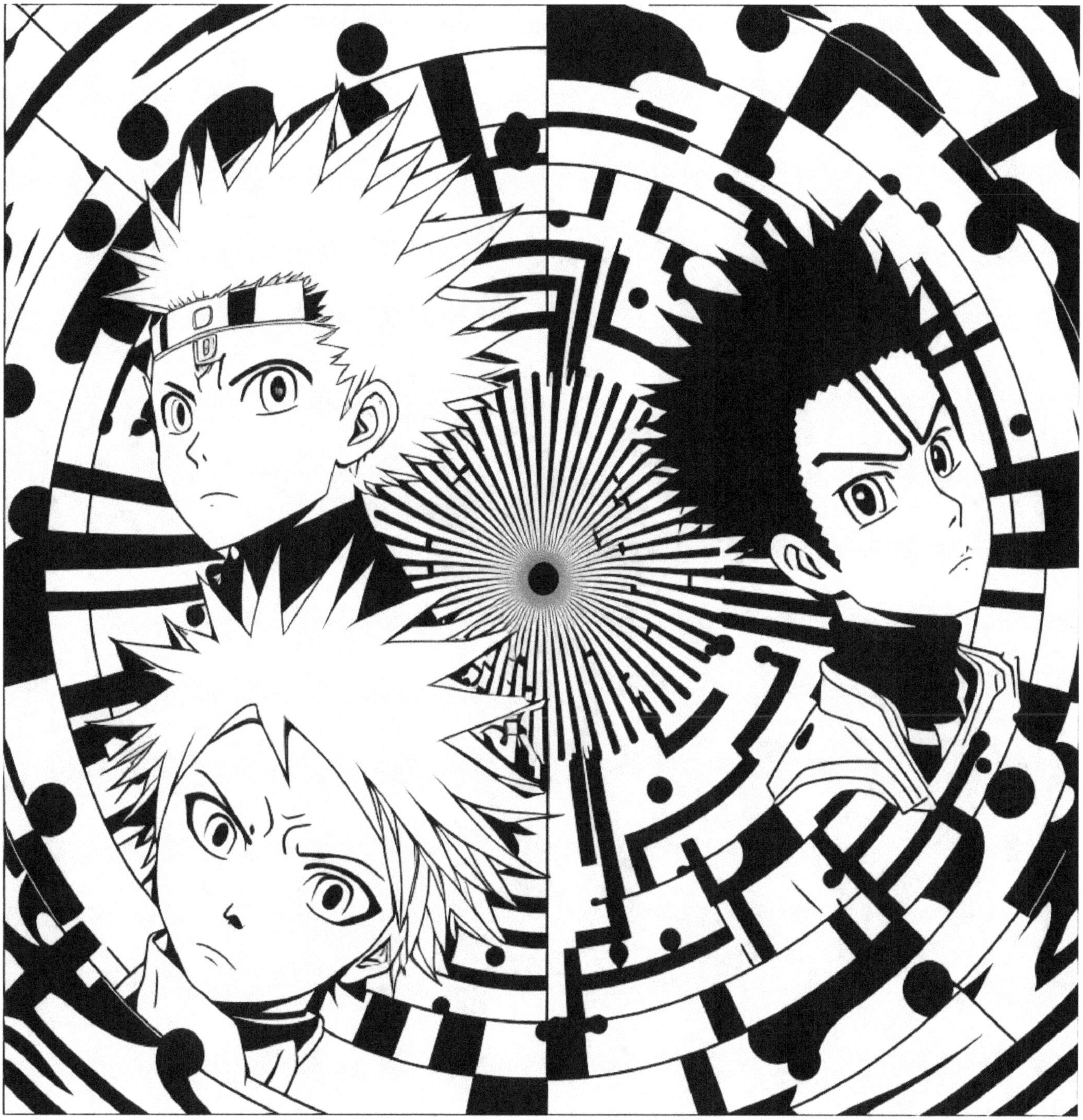

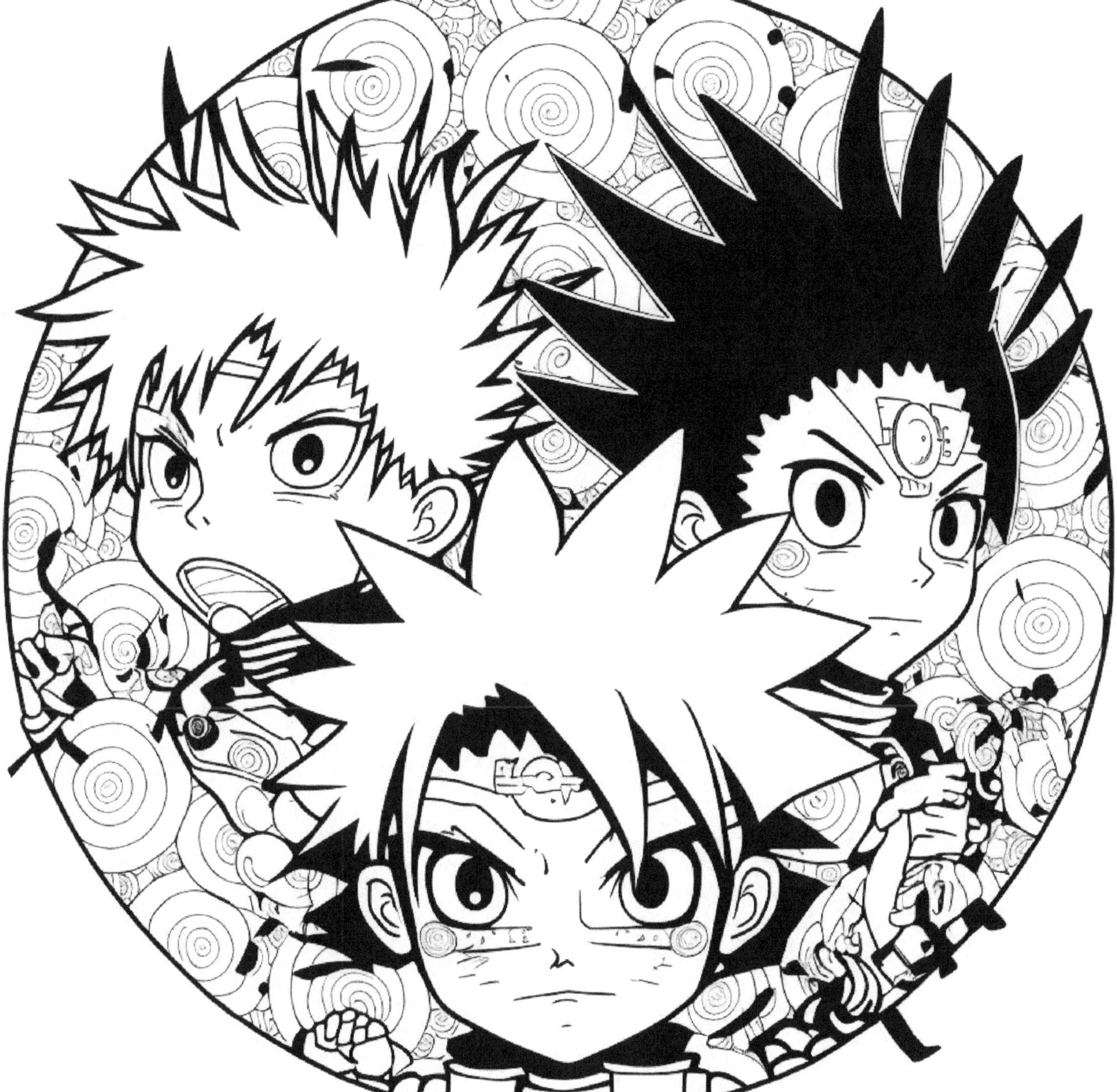

www.ingramcontent.com/pod-product-compliance
Lightning Source LLC
Chambersburg PA
CBHW080107010626
45794CB00015B/3299
* 9 7 9 8 8 6 8 4 8 8 6 4 1 *